Mahatma Gandhi

Leader of Indian Independence

Michael Nicholson

BLACKBIRCH™
PRESS

THOMSON
GALE

San Diego • Detroit • New York • San Francisco • Cleveland
New Haven, Conn. • Waterville, Maine • London • Munich

For more information, contact
The Gale Group, Inc.
27500 Drake Rd.
Farmington Hills, MI 48331-3535
Or you can visit our Internet site at http://www.gale.com

Photo Credits: Hulton Archive/Getty Images: cover; BBC Hulton Picture Library: 31, 42; Camera Press: 12, 26, 58, 59; Tom Hanley: 24, 25, 44, 52, 61; Indo-British Films Ltd: 20-1, 28-9, 32, 36-7, 40, 53, 57; the MacQuitty International Photographic Collection: 6 (top); National Army Museum: 15 (both), 30; National Gandhi Museum, New Delhi: 11, 13, 16, 19, 38 (below), 54, 56; Ann and Bury Peerless Slide Resources and Picture Library: 6 (below); the Photo Source: 4, 17, 43, 50, 55; Paul Popper Ltd: 38 (top), 48, 51; the Royal Commonwealth Society: 9 (both), 10; BK Sinha: 49. The map on page 62 is reproduced by kind permission of the Press Information Bureau, Government of India. Our grateful thanks go to Sir Richard Attenborough and Indo-British Films Ltd for permission to reproduce stills from the film *Gandhi*.

LIBRARY OF CONGRESS CATALOGING-IN-PUBLICATION DATA

Nicholson, Michael, 1937-
  Mahatma Gandhi / by Michael Nicholson.
    p. cm. — (World peacemakers series)
Summary: A biography of Mohandas K. Gandhi, who developed a system of non-violent civil disobedience while fighting racial discrimination in South Africa and India and eventually led his homeland to independence from Great Britain.
Includes bibliographical references and index.
  ISBN 1-56711-976-X (hardback : alk. paper)
  1. Gandhi, Mahatma, 1869-1948—Juvenile literature. 2. Statesmen—India—Biography—Juvenile literature. 3. Nationalists—India—Biography—Juvenile literature. [1. Gandhi, Mahatma, 1869-1948. 2. South Africa—History—19th century. 3. South Africa—History—20th century. 4. India—History—20th century. 5. India—Politics and government—1919-1947. 6. Statesmen.] I. Title. II. Series.

  DS481.G3N48 2004
  954.03'5'092—dc21 2003005138

Printed in China
10 9 8 7 6 5 4 3 2 1

Contents

The turning point

No one likes to feel unwanted. Nor do people like to receive insults and abuse from others. When Mohandas Gandhi, a young lawyer, traveled from his native India to South Africa on a business trip, he quickly learned that Indian people in that country were disliked, unwanted, and frequently insulted. Barbers refused to cut his hair. He was not allowed to stay in white hotels. He was attacked and beaten up by a stagecoach driver when he refused to give up his seat to a white passenger. A policeman forced him off a first-class railroad coach at the request of a white passenger who refused to share a compartment with a brown-skinned Indian.

After he was made to give up the seat for which he had a valid ticket, Gandhi had to spend the night in a freezing station waiting room. That night, he had plenty of time to consider his future as a new arrival in a hostile country. He had three options open to him. He could choose to ignore the insults and abuse and carry on with his work, he could go back to India, or he could stay and fight racial prejudice. Gandhi decided that it was his duty to stay and use his legal knowledge to fight for the black people and others of South Africa who faced racial discrimination.

Gandhi described this early experience in South Africa as a watershed—a turning point in his life. He was a changed man—and a man who was born to change history. Gandhi was forced to endure the hardship and humiliations that so many of his fellow countrymen had known all their lives. These experiences of injustice turned the shy twenty-four-year-old into a passionate fighter for human dignity and freedom. For the next fifty years, he fought injustice not with weapons, but with words and ideas, example and self-sacrifice. He developed *satyagraha*, a method of disciplined nonviolent civil disobedience. In South Africa, and later in India, he taught his followers to face British guns, bayonets, and *lathi* sticks with highly organized, unarmed passive resistance.

Indian leader Mohandas Gandhi fought for human rights in both his native India and in South Africa.

• •

"It has always been a mystery to me how men can feel themselves honored by the humiliation of their fellow beings."

—Mahatma Gandhi, in South Africa

• •

• •

"I discovered that as a man and an Indian I had no rights. More correctly, I discovered that I had no right as a man because I was an Indian."

—Mahatma Gandhi, in South Africa

• •

Gandhi's tomb is inscribed with the words "He Rama." The closest English translation is "Oh God." These were the words Gandhi spoke as he died.

Many Indians think of Gandhi as a great leader and a saint. Gandhi is memorialized in this statue outside the house where he was born.

When the protesters, including thousands of women, were attacked and brutally beaten, they did not strike back. The people made fair demands of those in power, and thousands were prepared to break unjust laws and go to jail.

Gandhi's teachings spread from South Africa to India and eventually throughout the world. Today, more than fifty years after his death, they still give people who are deprived of freedom and justice a way to fight oppression peacefully. Protest demonstrations and disciplined pressure are now viewed as effective ways to oppose what is wrong. Before Gandhi, though, the only way people knew how to fight oppression with any success was to fight and kill.

By the time of his death, Gandhi had led the Indian nation to independence. This gentle, smiling man was revered by hundreds of millions of Indians and by the leaders of the rest of the world as well. The United Nations (UN), in an unprecedented move, halted its deliberations when the news of his death reached New York. The UN recognized that Gandhi was a rare man indeed, a man whose influence would last far beyond his lifetime. The great scientist Albert Einstein said of Gandhi: "Generations to come, it may be, will scarcely believe that such a one as this ever in flesh and blood walked upon this earth."

Child of India

Mohandas Karamchand Gandhi was born in Porbandar, India, on October 2, 1869. In those days, India was ruled by the British. There were at the time more than 200 million people in India, at least seven times as many as lived in Great Britain and Ireland.

Gandhi was born into a land of contrasts: of desert plains, vast rivers, dense jungles, and the highest mountains on Earth. The climate of India is hot in the plains and cool in the highlands, but the vastness of the country creates great variety. India's peoples were separated from each other not only by

"Mahatma Gandhi will go down in history on a par with Buddha and Jesus Christ."

—Louis Mountbatten, the last British viceroy of India

"To observe at first hand that mighty effort, to rub up against, if ever so briefly, the towering greatness, the goodness, the high spirits and humor, the humility, the subtlety of mind, the integrity and purity of purpose, and that indefinable thing, the genius, of this man was the greatest stroke of fortune that ever befell me."

—William L. Shirer, Pulitzer Prize—winning author of *The Rise and Fall of the Third Reich*

the sheer difficulty of travel from one region to another, but also by different habits, religions, and more than three hundred languages. Even groups of peoples of the same race and religion were divided from one another by their caste, or station in life.

The British had been in India since the early seventeenth century, when they had first set up trading posts by force, bribery, or agreement with the Mogul emperor and the local princes who then ruled the country. The British ruled over many races: people in the south with very dark skin, and brown-skinned and pale-skinned people in the north. This was a land of princes, a land of great poverty and hunger but also of vast riches. In India, those who were rich had to do nothing for themselves. There was always a servant to wash, shave, or pour a cool drink for a wealthy master.

There were many different religions in India. Most people were Hindus, though of many different sects. The Muslims, who followed the teachings of the Prophet Muhammad found in the holy book of the Koran, were the second largest group. There were also Buddhists, who took their teachings from the Buddha, a religious thinker who lived twenty-five hundred years ago. A very old Christian church, whose faith was first brought to India by Saint Thomas, worshiped according to an ancient rite. Communities of Jews had also been in India for many centuries, along with tribal peoples from the hills and forests, and the Parsi, who originally came from Persia and worshiped fire as a symbol of God.

Hindus, who were mainly vegetarians, considered the cow to be sacred. Muslims, some of whom would eat beef, regarded the meat of pigs as unclean. A sect called the Jains believed all life forms were equally valuable, and covered their mouths so they would not swallow a fly. They would not go out at night for fear of treading on a worm. In striking contrast, white hunters—even those who might be devout Christians—took delight in hunting animals such as the graceful tiger, even near the point of extinction.

Opposite, top: English king George V, is shown on a hunting trip in 1911. Indian men aided him as he pursued the British tradition of hunting wild animals.

Opposite, lower: Gandhi grew up in an India ruled by the British. Tradition and ceremony played an important part in their rule of India from the early 17th century until 1947. This photo shows an example of one of the ceremonies the British favored while they ruled India.

In 1869, the year of Gandhi's birth, the ties between Great Britain and India drew closer. The Suez Canal was opened, and British ships no longer had to sail all the way around Africa to reach India. The grip of British power on India tightened. The links of trade were made even stronger. Because Great Britain had colonies across most of the world, it was said that "the sun never sets on the British Empire." It seemed then that the empire might last forever. Yet, over the course of Gandhi's life, the relationship between India and Great Britain changed dramatically, and the gentle Gandhi played a vital role in these important changes.

Boy bridegroom

Mohandas Gandhi was the fourth and last child of his father, Karamchand. Mohandas was born into the Vaisya caste, which was the second highest in Hindu society. Its members were below the most respected Brahmins (or priests) and the Kshatriyas, who were soldiers or rulers. Still, Gandhi's caste was much more privileged than the Sudra (worker) castes. Even worse off were those who were below all the others—those who had no caste—the untouchables or "outcasts." These were the people who carried out the most unpleasant, dirty tasks in Hindu society, such as cleaning the latrines. They were considered so lowly that caste Hindus thought they would be tainted if even their shadow was crossed by an untouchable. The untouchables were the people Gandhi later called the Harijan, or "Children of God."

Gandhi was a normal boy from a happy Hindu family, occasionally mischievous but no more than most. His father was a court official who became the first minister of the small princely state of Porbandar. His mother, Putlibai, was a very religious Hindu who prayed at each meal and often fasted. She often visited the temple and did not care for luxuries or jewels. His mother's religious life had a deep influence on the development of Gandhi's values.

Europeans had Indian servants who took care of all their needs. Here, a servant shaves his master.

Gandhi (shown here at age 7) was influenced at an early age by his deeply religious mother, Putlibai. His whole life was marked by the principles she taught him.

There were books at home, and life was comfortable enough. All the members of the family were strict vegetarians, but Gandhi was once persuaded by a Muslim boy to eat goat meat. The Muslim told Gandhi that meat would make him grow tall and strong—strong enough to push the British out of India. In the mistaken belief that he would grow stronger, Gandhi tried the meat. It gave him horrific nightmares, and later he deeply regretted the experiment.

Gandhi was a shy boy and he would often run home from school so that he did not have to speak to anyone. "I was always afraid lest anyone should poke fun at me," Gandhi remembered later. He loved to take long walks on his own and did not enjoy games.

When he was thirteen years old and still in school, Gandhi was married to Kasturba, the daughter of a

The youngest of four children, Gandhi (right) had a happy childhood. He is shown here, at age fourteen, seated with his older brother.

Porbandar merchant. He had not been consulted about the marriage. According to custom (which still survives in much of India today), the parents of the young couple made all the marriage arrangements, and the bride and groom did not meet until the wedding. Most Westerners today would probably wonder how such a marriage could possibly have a chance of success, but for Mohandas and Kasturba, it did not seem strange at all.

Student in the heart of the empire

In 1888, at the age of nineteen, Gandhi set out on a three-week voyage to London, where he was to study law. He was already a father: Harilal, his first son, had been born a few months earlier. Gandhi's student days were not particularly happy; he felt lonely, cut off from his family, and far from his spiritual home. He had sworn that, while in London, he would touch neither wine nor women, and would keep to his strict vegetarianism. Gandhi's moral principles alienated him from many of his fellow students, which made him feel even more isolated.

He wrote, "I would continually think of my home and country. . . . Everything was strange . . . the people, their ways and even their dwellings. I was a complete novice in the matter of English etiquette and had continually to be on my guard." His vegetarian diet made things even more difficult: "Even the dishes I could eat were tasteless and insipid."

Still, like most young people, Gandhi wanted to fit in as much as possible and to dress like his fellow students, so he went through a period in which he clothed himself in the fashions of the time. A fellow student recalled meeting Gandhi at Piccadilly Circus in London in 1890. Gandhi was "wearing a high silk top hat burnished bright, a stiff and starched white collar, a rather flashy tie displaying all the shades of the rainbow under which there was a fine striped silk shirt. He wore as his outer clothes a morning coat, a double-breasted waistcoat and dark striped trousers to match. . . . He also carried leather gloves and a silver-mounted stick." This was an extraordinary contrast with the Gandhi the world later came to know—the spiritual leader dressed in white homespun cloth, simple sandals, and a shawl.

After two years and eight months in England, Gandhi passed his final examinations at the Inner Temple Inn of Court in London and was called to the bar in June 1891. At twenty-two years of age, he had successfully completed his studies in French, Latin, physics, and common and Roman law. These studies helped train his mind but, though he was able and quick-witted, the young lawyer who sailed back from England did not yet possess the wisdom and resourcefulness that would eventually inspire millions. No one could have predicted that he would go

During his time studying law in London, Gandhi dressed in the European fashions of the time rather than in Indian-style clothing.

on to help free the largest colony in the British Empire and inspire millions of people. He himself referred to his college days as "the time before I began to live."

A new life in South Africa

On his return to India, Gandhi learned to his great sorrow that his mother had died. Gandhi had adored his mother and she had had a considerable influence on him. Shaped by her religious beliefs, Gandhi developed his own reverence for all forms of life and began to develop his beliefs about pacifism and non-violence.

For nearly two years, Gandhi tried to establish himself as a lawyer. His law practice was unsuccessful, though. When he stood up in court in Bombay to argue his first case, he became so nervous that he was unable to speak. He sat down to the sound of laughter in the courtroom. Shortly after this, Gandhi accepted an offer to represent a wealthy Indian merchant in South Africa.

South Africa at that time was deeply divided and troubled. Although black people outnumbered whites by more than five to one, they had few rights, and the nation was ruled by the tiny minority of whites. The whites were themselves divided. The British controlled the Natal and Cape colonies, while the Dutch Africans, or Boers, ruled the Transvaal and Orange Free State colonies. As a community, the approximately one hundred thousand Indian people in South Africa were despised. They had been imported to do the lowly and disagreeable jobs that no one else would do. These poor Indians, driven from home by semi-starvation, worked hard and lived in wretched poverty. A few did prosper, however, and they began to compete with the whites. For this, they became hated and feared. Numerous government rules and laws were put in place to attack the Indians and remove their right to vote, own land, and travel freely.

Gandhi, whose resolve was strengthened by his own experiences of racial injustice in his early days

14

15

This 1899 photograph shows Gandhi (center) with some of the ambulance men he led.

in South Africa, soon became a leader in the Indian community. By 1896, he was also a rich and successful lawyer.

Gandhi set about to help his people in very specific ways. Many of his ideas were practical and based on common sense. He tried to make the Indians appear friendlier and less strange to those of other races. He urged Indians to be honest in business so they would be trusted. He taught cleanliness and sanitation. He advised them to learn English so that they could talk to South Africans easily. He urged them to drop their ideas about caste, which separated one group of Indians from another.

Just before a trip back to India in 1896 to pick up his family, he wrote and published "The Green Pamphlet," which detailed Indian grievances in South Africa. This pamphlet was widely misinterpreted among whites as a call for Indians to rebel, and when he returned to South Africa in January 1897, Gandhi was attacked by a lynch mob. He escaped injury, and later clarified his views in a newspaper article, which helped calm tensions.

In 1899, the Boer War broke out between South Africa's Dutch and British colonies. Previously, Gandhi had taught Indians in South Africa that they should accept the obligations of citizenship. In other words, if the Indians wanted all the rights of subjects of the British Empire, they had to accept the same obligations as the empire's other subjects. The Boer War gave Gandhi the chance to put these ideas into action. He urged the Indian community to support the British. He helped form and train an Indian Ambulance Corps, and led one thousand ambulance men with distinction.

The British won the Boer War in May 1902. In December, Gandhi presented the Indian community's grievances to Joseph Chamberlain, the colonial secretary. Both Natal and the Transvaal were doing their best to drive Indians out. A new department was set up in the Transvaal in 1903, and it produced a stream of new rules and regulations over the next three years.

Gandhi (seated, center) lived in South Africa for twenty-one years. He ran a successful law firm in Johannesburg and was admired by the South African Indian community.

Tension grew between Indians and whites, although it eased somewhat during the Zulu Campaign of 1906. In this conflict, British troops fought against a tribe of black South Africans. Again, Gandhi helped the government by organizing another Indian Ambulance Corps. The corps marched many miles a day and cared for wounded Zulus whom the white doctors and nurses refused to touch.

The first struggles

In August 1907, the feelings of injustice in the Indian community came to a head. The Black Act required that all Indian men and women had to register and be fingerprinted. Anyone who did not could be imprisoned, fined, or deported. The Indians called these the "Black Laws" because they were unjust and aimed at nonwhites.

The Black Act spurred Gandhi to action. He organized a mass protest meeting that was attended by three thousand Indian men. In a speech, he explained the content of the Black Act, then he proposed that Indians refuse to obey the law and be ready to suffer the penalties. At the end of the meeting, as one, the audience members raised their arms over their heads and vowed to defy the Black Act.

The movement Gandhi now led employed what was often called passive resistance. Gandhi himself wanted a new word to describe his vision of nonviolent resistance, and he eventually settled on *satyagraha*, which meant "truth-force" or "love-force." It referred to "the vindication of truth not by the infliction of suffering on the opponent but on one's self." It requires self-control because the opponent must be "weaned from error by patience and sympathy." It is much more than "passive resistance," since it requires a constant positive interaction between the contestants.

The first test of *satyagraha* was the organized opposition to the Black Act. Most Indians simply refused to register and be fingerprinted at the offices the government had set up. Gandhi made strict rules about how his followers, the "Satyagrahis," should behave during this civil disobedience campaign. There was to be no retaliation for insults, floggings, or arrests. These were to be borne patiently. The idea was to humiliate opponents, not to fight them, but to melt their hearts.

In January 1908, because he had deliberately refused to register under the new law and had urged thousands of others to defy registration, Gandhi was sent to jail for two months. He did not complain, and was actually grateful to have time for peaceful thoughts and reading. In fact, he only served one month of the sentence.

The Black Act was not the only legislation that gave rise to nonviolent protest. Strict laws governed the freedom of Indians to enter the Transvaal. To test these unjust laws on immigration, many

Gandhi's wife, Kasturba, was photographed in 1903 with a nephew and three of their four children.

Indians crossed the Transvaal borders illegally. Gandhi did so and was jailed twice more. Whenever the Indians felt they were treated as second-class citizens, they quietly refused to cooperate and accepted their punishment.

In 1910, Britain formally unified the four colonies of the Transvaal, the Cape, the Natal, and the Orange Free State as the Union of South Africa. The government's hard-line treatment against Indians deepened. In an effort to harass Indians and induce them to leave the country, the Supreme Court of South Africa declared that all Indian marriages were invalid, a move that legally made all Indian children illegitimate and made all Indian wives mistresses without any rights.

For the first time, many women became involved in the civil disobedience campaign. The illegal border crossings into the Transvaal began again, and a group of women Gandhi called the "Natal Sisters" were arrested. Other Indian women from the Transvaal then made their way to Newcastle in Natal,

where they persuaded Indian miners to lay down their tools and go on strike. Many thousands of Indians were arrested and sent to jail and, as the word spread, thousands more workers went on strike.

By the time Gandhi called off the *satyagraha* campaign, he was known and respected throughout South Africa and India. The lawyer who had once been too shy to speak in court was now a famous statesman known for his honesty, skill, and courage.

In June 1914, Gandhi and General Jan Smuts, South Africa's minister of finance and defense, came together and worked out a give-and-take agreement

Gandhi told striking miners, who were charged by British troops, to lie down, as shown in this still from the movie Gandhi. *This action reflected one of the new methods of nonviolent civil disobedience he introduced while in South Africa.*

that gave the Indian community more dignity and self-respect. That same month, the Black Act was finally repealed. Gandhi's campaign of civil disobedience had triumphed, the first such campaign that would ever triumph.

Smuts pushed through the Indian Relief Act, and at last, after twenty years, Gandhi felt free to return home. When he left, he sent Smuts a pair of sandals he had made in prison. Smuts later said, "I have worn these sandals for many a summer since then, even though I may feel that I am not worthy to stand in the shoes of so great a man."

A fundamental change

Gandhi's time in South Africa had brought about many changes in him. For one thing, he had developed even more profound spiritual beliefs. He had always been a Hindu, but the principles of the Bhagavad Gita, the powerful Hindu book of scripture, had begun to permeate his life.

These beliefs greatly affected his politics. They also affected the way he dressed, the way he ate—indeed, every facet of his life. It was very difficult for non-Hindus to understand the principles Gandhi followed. Both in South Africa and later in India, the British misjudged his habits as eccentric.

Gandhi was influenced by other religions and philosophies: He particularly liked Christian hymns. He loved the teachings of Jesus Christ. Christ's Sermon on the Mount, Gandhi said, "went straight to the heart." The sermon included lessons such as "blessed are the meek," "blessed be the poor," "love your enemies," and "lay not up for yourselves treasures on earth." These teachings of Christ were at the very heart of Gandhi's way of life.

Gandhi borrowed freely from the principles of other religious groups, including Buddhists, Christians, Jains, and Muslims. In fact, partly because of this, he was an unorthodox Hindu and was often hated by strict Hindus. For Gandhi, one of the greatest principles was found in the Bhagavad Gita. It was called *Samakhava*, which meant that people should not allow themselves to be upset by either pain or pleasure. They should work for what is right without fear of failure or hope of success. Gandhi always laid as much stress on the means as on the end. He paid great attention on how to bring about change.

Another principle he followed was *Aparigraha*, which is nonpossession of material things. Spiritual riches could be reached through a poor and uncluttered way of life, without many goods.

Ahimsa, or nonviolence to all living things, is still another principle of Hinduism. This means noninjury to everything that lives. Because of this belief,

"... what did Gandhi teach me? I suppose the greatest single thing was to seek the truth, to shun hypocrisy and falseness and glibness, to try to be truthful to oneself as well as to others, to be skeptical of the value of most of life's prizes, especially the material ones, to cultivate an inner strength, to be tolerant of others ...

"... Also the necessity to discipline your mind and body and to keep your greeds and your lusts and your selfishness and your worldly ambitions in check; the obligation to love, to forgive and not to hate; to eschew violence and to understand the power of non-violence, grasping that the latter often demands more courage than the former."

—William L. Shirer, in *Gandhi, a Memoir*

Gandhi would not eat animals or hurt them in any way. He despised all violence and would not even kill, or allow to be killed, the deadly snakes that were sometimes found in the grounds around his home in South Africa. Instead, he would guide the snakes away with sticks.

Gandhi always sought truth and rejected anything hypocritical or false. He cultivated love and tolerance of other people and he was usually loved and deeply respected even by the people he opposed.

He was always able to be at peace because of his ability to meditate. Even when he was in tense negotiations or had to work under great pressure—with less than four hours of sleep a night—he was always cheerful, able to smile and joke.

Gandhi went through great changes in South Africa as he tried to discipline his body and mind and to keep his greed, selfishness, and desire for any kind of bodily pleasure in check. He had, for example, become extremely successful and wealthy because of his legal practice. He gave up all his wealth, however, including his home and fine clothes. He started an ashram, a communal farm. He even tried to give away his wife Kasturba's jewels—which had been given to the Gandhis as gifts by satisfied legal clients. Kasturba was especially upset with this decision of Gandhi's because, by tradition, her jewels would be needed as wedding gifts for her future daughters-in-law. Over the years, there were many other sacrifices that Gandhi demanded from his family and his growing band of followers.

Gandhi and Kasturba came to a mutual decision to take the vow of *Brahmacharya*. This means the complete cessation of all sexual activity. Gandhi felt that he had to rid himself of all physical desires in order to be at peace within himself and to be free under all circumstances, to help others and to act with love at all times. The nonviolent methods he pioneered and the political triumphs he had already achieved were based on these deep spiritual beliefs.

• •

"I have not the shadow of a doubt that any man or woman can achieve what I have, if he or she would make the same effort and cultivate the same hope and faith."

—Mohandas K. Gandhi

• •

This ashram, which Gandhi founded is still in operation today. Spinning is part of daily prayers there.

Gandhi comes home

In January 1915, when Gandhi was forty-five, he returned home to India. He and Kasturba, with their four young sons, were surprised to be met by huge crowds when they docked. News of Gandhi's achievements in South Africa had spread widely, and hundreds of Indians came to give him a warm welcome. The important people of Bombay held a grand reception in his honor.

Gandhi decided not to campaign for Indian rights until he had learned more about the problems in India. He did, however, set to work right away to establish his ashram at Sabarmati, near the city of Ahmedabad. The men and women of the community, eventually about two hundred of them, promised to live according to Gandhi's rules. These were based on the religious principles he had taught himself to live by when he was in South Africa. The residents'

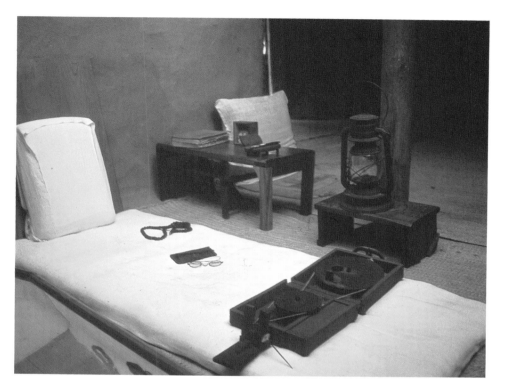

lives were to be marked by honesty, celibacy, and poverty. They would eat a modest vegetarian diet and lead a life of prayer and service to others.

Ashram life, with its many strict rules and lack of any type of luxury, might easily have become tedious for residents. Yet Gandhi was such a warm, loving person, and his beliefs so compelling, that people wanted to live with him and follow his ways. He was never short of followers.

Gandhi rapidly became known as a champion of the people's rights. He stuck up for the untouchables, the poor peasants, and factory workers in particular. He campaigned widely in early 1917 for the abolition of indentured workers who were sent to South Africa. Later the same year, he supported the indigo sharecroppers in Bihar against their British landlords, the farmers of Gujarat against taxes, and the mill-workers of Ahmedabad in a strike against their

This photograph shows Gandhi's bed and his belongings at the time of his death in 1948. His poverty and simplified way of life made it impossible for opponents to criticize him personally.

Gandhi and Kasturba returned to India in 1915. From then on, Gandhi did not wear Western clothing.

employers. He became so influential that later, in 1917, during the darkest days of World War I, he was summoned to Delhi. The viceroy, the British representative who ruled India, wanted Gandhi's assistance. To the great surprise of many pacifists, Gandhi agreed to call for Indian volunteers to fight for Great Britain and the empire.

Gandhi still believed that Great Britain was a force for good. He also believed, as he had in South Africa, that if the Indian people wanted rights as subjects of the empire, then they should serve the empire if asked to do so.

So volunteer Indian soldiers went to fight alongside British soldiers in World War I. The Indian soldiers fought in Mesopotamia and in Europe on the Western Front. Many died.

The Great War, as it came to be known, altered the course of history. The British and their allies finally won, but at a tremendous cost. Great Britain was severely weakened. Although few people thought so at the time, the days of the British Empire were numbered.

The Indian soldiers knew they had earned the right to dignity, equality, and self-respect. There seemed to be a new mood abroad. Yet the Indian soldiers were to be disappointed. During the war, Great Britain had come to an understanding with India, and had essentially promised the Indians self-government after the conflict was over. This agreement was not kept. Worse still, new laws gave the Indian colonial authorities emergency powers to clamp down on any so-called revolutionary activities. Trial without jury and imprisonment without trial were allowed. The Indian people felt cheated. It was obvious that the British did not intend to give up their most popular and profitable colony.

The first campaign

For the first time, Gandhi decided to go against the British government of India. To protest the unjust British laws, he decided to hold a *hartal*, a kind of general strike. He proclaimed a day when no business was to be done. Stores would stay shut. Employees would strike.

Across India, there was tremendous support for the *hartal*. Public protest, however, turned into riots in Delhi, Ahmedabad, Lahore, and Amritsar. Gandhi denounced the rioting troublemakers and called off the whole campaign. He saw that the people had to be trained in nonviolent obedience before civil disobedience could work. As penance for the violence his campaign had caused, Gandhi announced that he would fast for seventy-two hours. He asked others to fast for twenty-four hours.

The Amritsar Massacre

April 13, 1919, was India's blackest day. Three prominent English businessmen were killed by an angry mob in Amritsar. In response, the British dispatched military commander General Reginald Dyer to take control of the situation. Dyer immediately issued a proclamation that banned all public assembly in the town. But though the proclamation was read aloud in public places, the message failed to reach some parts of the city. When nearly twenty thousand unarmed Indians gathered in a large, vacant city lot, Dyer arrived on the scene. Without any warning to tell the crowd to disperse, he ordered a small force of native troops to fire into the unarmed gathering. The soldiers fired for ten minutes, and three hundred seventy-nine people were killed and more than twelve hundred wounded. At least some of the lives might have been saved if Dyer had not refused to allow Indian medics to tend to the wounded.

Dyer said later, "I thought I would be doing a jolly lot of good." To the Commission of Enquiry that investigated the incident, he said, "Yes, I think it quite possible that I could have dispersed them without firing, but I was going to punish them."

At Amritsar, Dyer also enforced the "Crawling Order." After an English missionary woman was injured, Dyer ordered that soldiers should be posted

"I believe that I have rendered a service to India and England by showing in non-cooperation the way out of the unnatural state in which both are living. In my humble opinion, non-cooperation with evil is as much a duty as is cooperation with good."

—Gandhi, speaking at his trial

with fixed bayonets along the street where she lived. The troops ensured that all Indians had to crawl along the whole street on their bellies. It did not matter if elderly men had to pass down the street to reach their homes; hundreds had to crawl in the dirt and dust. Most Indians—Gandhi included—felt thoroughly humiliated by this. It was something they would never forget.

Many British people, though not all, were deeply ashamed of Dyer's deeds and his various attempts to punish and shame the Indian people. The shock waves from the bloody Amritsar Massacre spread

At Amritsar, crowds gathered for a demonstration in sympathy with Gandhi's nonviolent hartal, *or* strike. *As shown in this photograph from the film* Gandhi, *troops opened fire and hundreds were killed.*

through all of India. The effect of Dyer's cruelty was to strengthen opposition to British rule. It also brought Gandhi into politics in a way he had never wanted to be before. He said, "I had faith in them [the British] until 1919, but the Amritsar Massacre and other atrocities in the Punjab changed my heart." For the first time, he began to see that British rule had to be overthrown. He returned his two British war medals and took on the leadership of the Indian nationalist movement. He realized that "self-rule" and "justice" were not enough. The British had to leave India entirely.

In June 1920, in protest against the policies of the British government, Gandhi returned the war medals he received while in South Africa.

Congress reform

Gandhi set about trying to accomplish the goal of independence through the Indian National Congress. Before Gandhi joined it, the congress was a group of middle-class men who made little real effort to oppose British rule. Gandhi breathed new life into the organization and rapidly became its acknowledged leader. He turned it into a powerful political party with branches all over the country, even in the villages.

In 1920, the congress passed Gandhi's resolution calling for *Swaraj*, or self-rule, if possible inside the British Empire (like the systems Canada and Australia had), but outside the empire if necessary. The congress called for the liberation of the untouchables and for the revival of village industries. Gandhi hated the way the untouchables were treated by the caste Hindus. He saw it as an insult and a threat to the Hindu religion. He wanted unity based on equality.

Spinning for victory

Gandhi viewed the revival of village industries, particularly weaving and spinning, as a way to alleviate the plight of the poor. He attributed the desperate poverty of the Indian villages to the town dwellers and the British textile mills, which had destroyed the village craft industry. India had once been self-sufficient in the production of *khadi*, a type of homespun cloth. Under British rule, however, Indians had begun to export raw materials to and import clothing from England. This had made the nation dependent on its colonial masters in order to clothe its people.

To change the situation, Gandhi urged Indians to discard their Western-style clothing and dress only in clothes that had been produced from cloth spun by Indians. In this way, the spinning wheel became the symbol of resistance to British rule. Under Gandhi's guidance, spinning became a moral duty, and homespun cloth became a symbol of self-sufficiency and independence.

Gandhi himself took a collapsible spinning wheel everywhere he went, and he often spun yarn as he spoke to the crowds. The wheel's gentle hum could be heard at congress meetings or wherever nationalists gathered. For the rest of his life, Gandhi spun two hundred yards of yarn every single day. Even if he was at an international conference or worked until 2:00 A.M., he would not sleep until he had spun his daily quota.

During 1921, Gandhi went all over India—in third-class railway compartments—to spread the message that noncooperation would lead to independence. At vast public meetings, he urged the people not to wear foreign clothing and to boycott British cloth.

His followers would strip off their foreign-made clothes and throw them into a fire, and volunteers picketed stores that sold British cloth. By this time, Gandhi himself had permanently adopted his famous loincloth and carried a homespun bag. Sometimes, Gandhi's followers took their protest farther than Gandhi would have liked. For example, at times, merchants' stock of foreign clothing were set

As part of a boycott of British goods, Gandhi urged Indians to spin their own cloth. No matter how busy he was, Gandhi spun two hundred yards of yarn every day.

In a scene from the movie Gandhi, a group of Gandhi's followers set fire to a police station and kill twenty-two policemen at Chauri Chaura in 1921. After this incident, Gandhi gave up his civil disobedience campaign.

alight and the fires of burning warehouses lit the sky at night. Gandhi did not approve of such actions.

In October 1921, a congress working party called for a strike. Soldiers and civil servants were asked to desert their posts. Lawyers were urged to give up their practices, and many did so. Schools and colleges were disrupted. More and more villages refused to pay taxes. By December, twenty thousand people had been imprisoned for civil disobedience and sedition.

The country was in a state of great excitement. Chaos was the order of the day. Amidst the expressions of pacifism and high ideals, though, there was growing disorder and violence on the streets. Even the British, who knew India well, were bemused and bewildered by the leading revolutionary activists, and especially by Gandhi. The gentle, middle-aged Gandhi, dressed in a loincloth and usually smiling, now attracted crowds of thousands of excited supporters wherever he went. They would walk for days just to see their great leader. As the situation came to the boil, rioting and disorder spread. Gandhi fasted as a penance for the violence. Then, in February 1921, in the Chauri Chaura (United Provinces), twenty-two police constables were killed by an enraged mob during a campaign of mass disobedience. Gandhi was sickened by the atrocity and stopped the defiance of the government everywhere in India.

"It is better," said Gandhi, "to be charged with cowardice and weakness than to be guilty of denial of our oath and to sin against God. It is a million times better to appear untrue before the world than to be untrue to ourselves."

Many of Gandhi's followers were disappointed. Many felt let down or betrayed. Despite their disapproval of his decision, Gandhi was not prepared to sacrifice the principle of nonviolence.

The first stage of the struggle was at an end. It had made some significant achievements. The Indian National Congress had flexed its muscles and demonstrated its power. It had become obvious that hundreds of thousands of people were prepared to make great sacrifices, to give up their jobs, and risk imprisonment for the cause of freedom. This success only convinced Gandhi that for nonviolence to succeed, his supporters had to be highly trained and much more disciplined. He himself went on a five-day fast to seek atonement for the murders in Chauri Chaura. For the British government of India, recent events showed that the Indian National Congress could no longer be ignored. The demands of Indian nationalism had to be recognized and in some way satisfied. The nationalists themselves felt more able to deal with the British government on equal terms.

Arrest and imprisonment

Shortly after the killings at Chauri Chaura, in March 1922, Gandhi was arrested. He was charged with rebellion against the government. At his trial, Gandhi, who described himself as a farmer and

"I came reluctantly to the conclusion that the British connection had made India more helpless than she was before, politically and economically. India has become so poor that she has little power of even resisting famines. Before the British advent, India spun and wove in her millions of cottages just the supplement she needed for adding to her meager agricultural resources. This cottage industry, so vital to India's existence, has been mined by incredibly heartless and inhuman processes . . . the profits and the brokerage are sucked from the masses."

—Mohandas K. Gandhi

33

weaver, pled guilty. He made a long statement in which he said, "the section under which I am charged is one under which mere promotion of disaffection is a crime. I have studied some of the cases under it, and I know that some of the most loved of India's patriots have been convicted under it. I consider it a privilege, therefore, to be charged under that section. . . . I hold it to be a virtue to be disaffected toward a government which in its totality has done more harm to India than any previous system. India is less manly under the British rule than she ever was before. Holding such a belief, I consider it a sin to have affection for the system.

"I am here therefore to invite and submit to the highest penalty that can be inflicted upon me for what in law is a deliberate crime and what appears to me to be the highest duty of a citizen."

Gandhi did receive the maximum sentence of six years, and he went cheerfully to prison again. He told the trial judge he was grateful for the courtesy he had received during the trial. He had no regrets. "We must widen the prison gates," he said. "Freedom is to be wooed only inside prison walls." Happy in his prison cell, Gandhi spent his time at peace with his books, his spinning wheel, and his prayers. He was released in 1924 after he had to have an operation for acute appendicitis.

When Gandhi came out of prison, he discovered that the Indian National Congress was in disarray. The noncooperation movement had collapsed. Even worse, there was much community unrest and bitterness between Muslims and Hindus. Three-quarters of the Indian people were Hindus, and their religion had survived through wars, foreign conquest, and occupation. Yet Muslims had ruled India for centuries, although they had left Hinduism basically untouched.

Gandhi chose not to renew his campaign of civil disobedience until his prison sentence would have been fully served. Instead, he devoted much of the next few years to an effort to bring Hindus and Muslims together.

"We did not conquer India for the benefit of the Indians. We conquered India as the outlet of goods of Great Britain. We conquered India by the sword, and by the sword we should hold it."

—Lord Brentford, 1930

In these quiet years, Gandhi continued to preach the virtues of the spinning wheel and the handloom. Gandhi said the wheel was like a restful prayer. He was accused of fanaticism but he persisted anyway. He repeated his view that the great British textile mills and the Indian cities had made the Indian countryside poor. Gandhi urged his people to wear *khadi*, or homespun cloth. If they bought *khadi* instead of British cloth, the townspeople would help the peasants. Homespun cloth would form the link between town and country, rich and poor. The India of jewels and riches and silver and gold brocade was not Gandhi's India. Homespun became the badge of the nationalists.

Civil disobedience

In 1928, Gandhi, now fifty-nine years old, turned again to the liberation of India. Gandhi won the support of many doubters because of the sense of his position. He pointed out that more than 80 percent of Indians were peasants—to win their support, it was essential to speak their languages, dress like them, and understand their economic requirements and aspirations. They were far more likely to listen to an old man in a *khadi* loincloth and sandals who spoke their own language, than to a Europeanized congress member who spoke in English.

Gandhi traveled throughout India. He spoke at rallies and organized bonfires of foreign cloth. Then, at a December 1928 meeting of the Indian National Congress, Gandhi was among the leaders who endorsed a daring and potentially risky new resolution. It said that if Britain did not grant India the status of an independent British Commonwealth nation by the end of 1929, the congress would organize a countrywide campaign of noncooperation. Indians everywhere would be encouraged to refuse to pay their taxes, and that surely would bring the government grinding to a halt.

A pinch of salt

On December 31, 1929—the deadline the Indian National Congress had given the British for granting

"Yes, but we have something more important than guns. We have truth and justice—and time—on our side.

You cannot hold down much longer three hundred and fifty million people who are determined to be free. You will see!"

—Mohandas K. Gandhi

35

India its independence—India was still firmly under British rule. Most congress leaders wanted to carry through their threat to launch a campaign of noncooperation and refusal to pay taxes; however, they had not yet reached agreement on exactly how to organize the protests or on which taxes to target. They turned to Gandhi to come up with an effective plan.

On March 1, Gandhi delivered a letter to the British viceroy, Lord Irwin, in which he detailed why he felt the British system was crushing the life out of the Indian people. A perfect example of British tyranny, Gandhi wrote, were the British salt laws, which made it a punishable crime for Indians to make their own salt or possess salt not purchased from government factories. The tax hit the poor the hardest, since

no one, particularly in a hot country, can live without salt. The poorest peasant had to pay as much as the richest merchant. Many people also believed that to charge money for a substance that nature provided free was repugnant.

The viceroy did not respond to the letter, so on March 12, Gandhi, along with seventy-eight followers, began to march from his Sabarmati ashram to the coast of the Arabian Sea, some two hundred miles away. By the time they arrived, several thousand villagers had joined them. The climax of the march was when Gandhi stooped to pick up a few grains of salt left by the waves. It was a simple act, but it symbolized the defiance of hundreds of millions of Indians against the world's strongest colonial power.

Though he knew how dangerous the power of such a demonstration could be, Gandhi planned the twenty-four-day, two-hundred-mile Salt March (shown in this movie still from Gandhi*).*

Above: During the Salt March, Gandhi (second from left) walked next to the poet Sarojini Naidu. She later led demonstrators to the Dharasana Saltworks after Gandhi was imprisoned.

Right: When Gandhi scooped up a handful of salt, the symbolic gesture started a nationwide outbreak of civil disobedience.

The British treated the march as a joke and dismissed the whole idea. They did not see what was so dramatic about picking up a bit of salt. Once again the British underestimated Gandhi. They did not understand the feelings that now ran through India and they certainly had no understanding of how formidable and clever Gandhi would be now that he was an outright opponent of the government.

Gandhi's flouting of the salt tax law gripped people's imaginations. Civil disobedience broke out in nearly every province. All over India, poor people began to take salt from the sea. At least sixty thousand people were arrested, including nearly all the Indian National Congress leaders.

On the night of May 5, Gandhi himself was arrested. He had been asleep under a mango tree near the seashore. The police came with guns. Gandhi was quite calm. He brushed his teeth with a twig in the Indian way and allowed the police to take him away. There was no trial and no sentence—he was simply put in jail. Gandhi had relied on the assumption that he would be arrested; it was all part of his strategy for the salt march.

Satyagraha in action

Protests continued after Gandhi's imprisonment. Sarojini Naidu, a poet, led twenty-five hundred congress volunteers to the Dharasana Saltworks. This plant was defended by policemen armed with steel-shod staves. After prayers, the protesters moved forward. The first column was headed by one of Gandhi's four sons, Manilal. They were viciously attacked and beaten by the soldiers. In accordance with the rules of nonviolence, they did not defend themselves. They fell where they stood as blows rained on their heads with sickening thuds. As the wounded fell with fractured skulls and concussions, they were dragged away by women protesters. A second column came forward and approached the stockade in complete silence. A British officer barked an order, and the police beat the protesters down.

> "... As we saw the abounding enthusiasm of the people and the way salt-making was spreading like a prairie fire, we felt a little abashed and ashamed for having questioned the efficacy of this method when it was first proposed by Gandhi. And we marveled at the amazing knack of the man to impress the multitude and make it act in an organized way."
>
> —Jawaharlal Nehru, leader of Congress and later India's first prime minister

They were dragged away. A new column formed: "They marched steadily, with heads up, without the encouragement of music or cheering or any possibility that they might escape serious injury or death. The police rushed out and methodically and mechanically beat down the column. There was no fight, no struggle; the marchers simply walked forward till struck down." This was repeated, hour after hour. Two men died and three hundred twenty were injured.

The dreadful scene was witnessed by Webb Miller, an American journalist, whose horrific account was published in more than one thousand newspapers. It did much to stir the conscience of Great Britain and the world about what was happening in India. Yet again, *satyagraha* was succeeding. The more unjust and cruel the British were, the more they played into Gandhi's hands.

Within a year, Gandhi was invited to the viceroy's palace, where he negotiated with viceroy Lord Irwin, the representative of the British government. The series of talks resulted in what was known as the Irwin-Gandhi Pact. Among other things, the agreement permitted the free manufacture of salt. Civil disobedience was called off, prisoners were to be released, and the Indian National Congress was to be represented at the Round Table Conference in London, the second of two meetings Parliament held to discuss the future of India.

The Round Table Conference

In August 1931, Gandhi sailed for Great Britain as the sole representative of the Indian National Congress. On embarkation, Gandhi warned, "I might come back empty handed." He did not hold out much hope for the conference. In truth, he was not very interested in the details of how a new Indian government should work. His was the human approach and, at the human level, he scored a great success. He conquered the hearts of many British men and women and persuaded many more of the justice of his cause.

This scene from the movie Gandhi *shows the Dharasana Saltworks where 2,500 demonstrators faced 400 Indian policemen. For hours, row after row of protesters were beaten without fighting back. Two men died and 320 were injured.*

. . . .

"Europe has completely lost her former moral prestige in Asia. She is no longer regarded as the champion throughout the world of fair dealing and the exponent of high principle, but as the upholder of western race supremacy and the exploiter of those outside her own borders."

—Rabindranath Tagore, Indian writer, who first called Gandhi the "Mahatma (Great Soul) in peasants' garb"

. . . .

. . . .

"All hope of reconciling India with the British Empire is lost forever. I can understand any government taking people into custody and punishing them for breaches of the law, but I cannot understand how any government that calls itself civilized could deal as savagely and brutally, with nonviolent, unresisting men as the British have this morning."

—V. J. Patel, leader of the *swaraj* (self-rule) during Gandhi's arrest

. . . .

Newspaper headline writers loved him. When asked whether he had felt sufficiently clothed when he visited the king, he said, "The King had enough on for both of us." The English were intrigued by details of Gandhi's personal habits, his dress, and his diet.

When he ventured into the cotton towns of Lancashire to explain why he had started the boycott of British cloth, Gandhi was cheered by the workers, many of whom were unemployed because of his policy. They liked the fact that Gandhi had taken the trouble to come and talk with them. This was something their own rulers rarely, if ever, did.

"Do you want your own prosperity to be built on the misery of others?" Gandhi asked them. They said no. He told them that they were much better off with the unemployment pay they received every week than an Indian worker, who got less than half of that amount per month when he was actually working.

Gandhi was not a materialist. He did not value wealth, but he hated grinding, desperate poverty. He said, "No sophistry, no jugglery in figures can explain away the evidence that the skeletons in many villages present to the naked eye. I have no doubt that both England and the town dwellers in India will have to answer, if there is a God above, for this crime against humanity which is perhaps unequalled in history. . . .

"My ambition is no less than to convert the British people through nonviolence and thus make them see the wrong they have done in India. I do not seek to harm your people. I want to serve them even as I want to serve my own."

Gandhi's personal triumph was tremendous, but the conference itself was a failure. In fact, it was worse than a failure because it widened the differences between the Indians themselves. As Gandhi put it, "They went into the conference Muslims and Sikhs and Untouchables, and they came out of it Muslims and Sikhs and Untouchables—and never at any moment was the Indian nation there."

Gandhi, dejected but determined, left for India. He would never again return to Great Britain.

While he was in England, Gandhi's native clothing attracted attention. British leaders, however, were more interested in his impressive negotiating skills.

A new fast

Within three weeks of Gandhi's return to India, he was again jailed. A new viceroy, Lord Willingdon, had been put in charge. In a crackdown on the nationalist movement, he declared the INC an illegal organization, confiscated its funds, and jailed its leaders, including Gandhi.

In prison, Gandhi learned that the British were working to create separate political parties: one for the Hindus, one for the Muslims, and a third for the untouchables. Under the system, Hindus could only vote for Hindus, Muslims could only vote for Muslims, and untouchables could only vote for untouchables. Gandhi detested this proposal. He knew that Hindus and Muslims were often deeply divided on many issues, so he reluctantly agreed to separate political parties for these two groups. Separating the untouchables from the Hindus, how-

Though hundreds of thousands of cotton workers lost their jobs because of Gandhi's boycott of British cloth, he was still cheered by workers when he visited cotton towns in Lancashire, England, in 1931.

Gandhi thought the caste system was the worst aspect of Hinduism. He campaigned for improvements to the way of life of the lowest caste, the untouchables (pictured).

ever, was too much for him. He felt that the untouchables should be integrated into the Hindu castes.

Gandhi decided that to protest the proposed system, he would refuse to eat until the Hindus and the untouchables agreed on a more unified voting arrangement. With Gandhi's life at stake, an agreement was worked out. More important than voting rights, however, was the fact that Gandhi's fast helped improve the lot of the untouchables. They were not only touched but even embraced by their fellow Hindus. Wells and temples where they had not been allowed to go were now opened to them. After his release from prison in 1933, Gandhi set out on a twelve-thousand-mile tour to collect money for the untouchables.

Gandhi was a very religious Hindu, and he believed that if someone led a bad life, he or she would come back to life as a member of an inferior caste. Gandhi would not accept untouchability, however. As he said, "I know of no argument in favor of untouchability . . . indeed I would reject all authority if it is in conflict with sober reason or the dictates of the heart."

Gandhi began to work constantly on an issue that was central to him—Hindu-Muslim unity. The two groups had begun to drift further apart, and Gandhi was heartbroken. He could see that independence would probably cause the final split. He always said that independence should be delayed if there was any chance of avoiding that final rift.

Storm clouds of war

If there was ever any doubt that the British would be forced to leave India within a few years, the start of World War II in 1939 settled the matter. On the whole, leaders of India's congress (which had been allowed to start meeting again) supported Great Britain in the fight, but they resigned when the viceroy declared without consulting them that India was also at war. To try to win congress over, the British promised independence after the war. Despite this, Gandhi still refused to support the British war effort. He insisted on independence at once.

In August 1942, Gandhi called upon the British to "Quit India." He told the All India Congress Committee, "Our quarrel is not with the British people, we fight their imperialism." Perhaps Gandhi did not fully understand the significance of his action. Dreadful riots followed his "Quit India" demand.

Kasturba's death

Violence broke out again all over India when, two days after his "Quit India" speech, Gandhi was arrested and imprisoned yet again. This was a time of great personal tragedy for Gandhi. Within a few days of his arrest, his devoted secretary, Mahadev

"To see the universal and all-pervading spirit of truth face to face one must be able to love the meanest of creatures as oneself."

—Gandhi, in his autobiography

"I hold myself to be incapable of hating any being on earth. By a long course of prayerful discipline, I have ceased for over forty years to hate anybody. I know this is a big claim. Nevertheless, I make it in all humility."

—Mohandas K. Gandhi

Desai, died suddenly. Then, his wife became ill. Gandhi and Kasturba, whom he called Ba, spent the last months of their lives together in prison. Their relationship, which had often been difficult when they were young, had mellowed as they grew older. Kasturba had come to be a significant influence on Gandhi's life, even if she remained in the background. When death came, it was Gandhi who held her. Gandhi said, "I can say of the vacuum that has been created by Ba's death, it is something very different, a vacuum which cannot be filled." Ba had borne Gandhi four sons. They had been together since they were children.

Six weeks after his wife's death, Gandhi was released from prison. He was very ill, and the viceroy feared more violence would come if he died in jail.

The transfer of power

The Allied victory in 1945 at the end of World War II marked the beginning of the end of colonialism. Great Britain was exhausted, and the new Labor Party government was committed to Indian independence.

In 1945, the other Indian National Congress leaders were released from prison. In the elections that followed, congress kept its position as the largest political party, but it no longer spoke for the Muslims. During the war, with congress leaders in prison, the Muslim League, led by Muhammad Ali Jinnah, had gained increasing support for the creation of a separate Muslim state of Pakistan. The idea of "partition"—a division of India—was despised by Gandhi and the congress.

Great Britain's new Labor government decided to make one last attempt to preserve Indian unity. A cabinet mission was sent out to Delhi in 1946. Negotiations dragged on for three months, but finally broke down because congress and the Muslim League did not trust each other.

The viceroy, Lord Wavell, invited Gandhi's disciple Jawaharlal Nehru to form an interim (temporary) government. Nehru asked Jinnah for assistance to help run the government. He also offered the Muslim League several government posts. Jinnah was unable to agree.

In August, the Muslim League decided upon a "Direct Action Day" as a protest against "Congress Government" and to force the British to recognize Muslim demands for a separate state. This led to a fearful outbreak of violence in the Calcutta region. Four thousand people were killed and fifteen thousand injured in a wave of shootings, stabbings, and burnings. The bloodshed and murder spread to East Bengal. Muslim gangs killed and forcibly converted Hindus.

The news horrified Gandhi, who decided to go "to bury myself in East Bengal until such a time as the Hindus and Muslims learn to live together in peace. . . . I do not know," he said, "what I shall be able to do there. All that I know is that I won't be at peace unless I go."

Gandhi described this mission as the most difficult in his whole life. When a colleague went to visit Gandhi in East Bengal, he found him in the house of a *dhobi*, a village washerman. "So there he was in the little hut of the village washerman, writing his letters by the light of a kerosene lamp." People found it heartbreaking to see the frail little man, now seventy-seven years old, as he walked barefoot from village to village. Gandhi threw every effort into his supreme task. He held prayer meetings and preached courage, forgiveness, and truth.

From Bengal, Gandhi went to Bihar, where the victims of the riots were Muslims rather than Hindus. By March, Gandhi was holding prayer meetings, and collecting money from Hindus for Muslim relief. He stayed in a small Muslim village, went on a half-fast, and vowed that he would not leave until Muslims and Hindus were at peace. One month later, the killings stopped.

The last viceroy

The continuing disorder in India, despite Gandhi's efforts, made the British government fearful. Jinnah

• •

"The welcome was so disarming, his manner so friendly and radiant, that my nervousness evaporated before I could say a word.

". . . His gray eyes lit up and sharpened when they peered at you through his steel-rimmed spectacles and they softened when he lapsed, as he frequently did, into a mood of puckish humor. I was almost taken back by the gaiety in them. This was a man inwardly secure, who, despite the burdens he carried, the hardships he had endured, could chuckle at man's foibles, including his own."

—William L. Shirer, in *Gandhi, a Memoir*

• •

This photo shows a riot in Bombay, a scene of Hindu-Muslim violence. Though half a million died during India's move to independence, it is believed that without Gandhi's leadership, a full-scale civil war may have developed.

still held out for partition, and the resolve of congress had begun to weaken. Worried that an agreement might never be reached and horrified at the prospect of civil war, British prime minister Clement Attlee made a bold decision: The British would hand over power to the Indians no later than June 1948. The new and final viceroy appointed to carry out the job was Lord Louis Mountbatten. He had been a World War II commander and was a cousin of King George VI. Mountbatten came to the job youthful, informed, and with complete authority. He arrived in Delhi in March 1947, and almost immediately, he sent word to Gandhi that he wished to see him.

Mountbatten said he would send a plane to pick him up, but Gandhi insisted on going to Delhi in a third-class railway compartment. The first meeting with Gandhi was something of a surprise for Mountbatten. He recalled, "Certainly I was quite unprepared to meet such a lovable old man, with a warm, human manner; great good humor; charming manners; and perhaps most unexpectedly of all, an unfailing sense of humor. My wife and I welcomed him together, and friendly relations were effortlessly established."

Time was short. Mountbatten said, "I could sense a real tragedy round the corner if we didn't act very fast—civil war in its worst form. Beside that, Partition, much as many of us hated it, seemed a much lesser evil. I could see no alternative." Partition was inevitable, and this also meant that two important regions with large Muslim populations would have to be divided: Bengal in the east and the Punjab in the west.

Mountbatten's team worked around the clock to produce an independence plan in six weeks. Muhammad Ali Jinnah was not enthusiastic about it. Although he had insisted on partition, he was not satisfied with what he called his "moth-eaten

Gandhi went to East Bengal to stop the killing of Hindus by Muslims. He moved from village to village to preach courage and try to calm the people.

Lord Louis Mountbatten (top, left) was appointed to finalize India's independence from Britain. He realized that Gandhi's support would be important for a peaceful changeover.

Pakistan." The main argument was over Bengal and the Punjab. Jinnah had insisted on partition. He believed that without it, the Muslims would be swamped in Hindu India. Mountbatten and congress said, "By the same argument, the two provinces you want in Pakistan, with large non-Muslim minorities, will also have to be partitioned."

When it came, independence came fast. Many said it was too fast. Pakistan became a country made up of two parts that were separated by more than eight hundred miles. Later, in 1971, the eastern part of Pakistan, East Bengal, broke away in a rebellion to form the independent nation of Bangladesh.

Partition

For many of India's people, August 15, 1947, was one of the greatest days in history. One-fifth of the population of the world won independence that day. All the quarrels and animosities that had built up between the Indians and the British over the decades seemed to melt away. There was great rejoicing.

With Lord Mountbatten's wife, Lady Edwina, by his side, Gandhi entered the Viceroy's House for independence negotiations. Gandhi tried to prevent the partition of India into separate Muslim and Hindu countries.

Gandhi found nothing to celebrate, however. He felt what he called "Partition of the Heart." "My independence," he said, "has not yet come . . . there is no reason for festivals and merriments like this." Gandhi's ideal of unity, for which he had fought all his life, had been rejected. He felt deserted by his fellow countrymen, and abandoned by the colleagues and friends he had loved.

Gandhi had always said he would like to live to be 125 years old. Now, as the violence mounted and Hindus and Muslims started to kill each other, he said at his prayer meetings: "I wanted to be 125. Now I

Though Gandhi fought forty years for India's freedom, he did not celebrate on August 15, 1947, when independence was granted. He was working for peace between Hindus and Muslims even as celebrations, such as this one in Delhi, took place.

have lost interest in life." Even in these last months of his life, though, Gandhi still had more battles to fight.

"The old man has done it again!"

August 1947 found Gandhi in Calcutta. Although he felt sad and rejected himself, Gandhi could still bring courage, comfort, and forgiveness to others. Calcutta had already been through a year of terrible violence before Gandhi arrived. A well-known Indian writer, Sudhin Datta, remembered later, "For a year it had seemed as if it was not worth living in Calcutta. And then Gandhi had come. The first day I think they threw brickbats at him, and sticks at him, and then of course he talked to them, and slowly in two or three days time the atmosphere changed and on the 14th what we saw is perhaps the only miracle I have seen in my life."

The "miracle" occurred as Muslims and Hindus began to dance and celebrate together, and soldiers had little flags on their bayonets pinned on by the

crowd. People said, "The old man has done it again!"

Still, Gandhi could not celebrate. By the end of the month, violence again erupted, and Gandhi himself barely escaped injury. He told the people he would start a fast in Calcutta that would end only when the violence ended. Within four days, the chief citizens of Calcutta brought him written promises of peace by their peoples, and Gandhi was able to break his fast.

This movie still from Gandhi *shows people uprooting their lives after independence was declared. Millions of people moved: Muslims left India for the newly created country of Pakistan, and Hindus left Pakistan for India.*

One-man boundary force

That was in Bengal. In the Punjab, in the north, where the authorities had also expected riots, fifty-five thousand soldiers were stationed. They were overwhelmed by the violence and by the number of people who were forced to leave their homes. Then Gandhi arrived. As Mountbatten said later, "When the trouble started the 55,000-man boundary force in the Punjab was swamped by riots, but my one-man boundary force brought peace in Bengal."

In September, Gandhi undertook his last journey—back to Delhi. The capital city was ablaze with communal strife. There was murder and bloodshed. Refugees fled from the old walled city as others poured in. This was just a small part of the mass movement of peoples that took place all over northern India. No one really knows how many lives were lost in those tragic weeks of violence, but estimates of two hundred thousand are probably too low. More than 15 million fled from India to Pakistan or in the opposite direction.

Gandhi set to work. "I must do what I can to calm the heated atmosphere," he said. He visited the refugee camps; some housed Sikhs and Hindus who had been driven out of the Punjab; some contained Muslims chased out of their homes in Delhi. Gandhi's platform was the daily prayer meeting, which was usually held in the garden of Birla House where he stayed. His preaching and readings from

While troops could not stop the violence in East Bengal, Gandhi, by preaching his method of nonviolence, brought peace to the area.

the Hindu Bhagavad Gita, the Muslim Koran, and the Jewish-Christian Bible were an inspiration. Hundreds attended, and often, thousands more listened on the radio.

The last fast

Prayer was not enough. Gandhi felt he had to do more. In January 1948, he announced his intention to begin a fast to the death. "The fast will end," he said, "when I am satisfied that there is a reunion of hearts of all communities." This, at the age of seventy-eight, his eighteenth great fast, was to be the final fast of his life.

By the third day of the fast, the Indian government was persuaded by Gandhi to make a considerable payment of money due to Pakistan. Many Hindus were outraged. They thought Gandhi was fasting to assist the Muslims who were at war with India in the Kashmir region. Crowds of refugee Hindus demonstrated outside Birla House. They chanted, "Blood for Blood" and "Let Gandhi die."

Gandhi was finally satisfied by the pledges given to him by the leaders of the different communities in Delhi. These representatives promised to restore communal peace and friendship by every possible effort, even at the cost of their own lives. Gandhi broke his fast on the sixth day.

Gandhi did not spare himself. He took no time to recover from the fast before he went back to work. He began to work furiously on plans to give power to the people, and on many of his old ideas about putting life back into the villages. In the evenings, he held the usual prayer meetings. At one of these, shortly after Gandhi broke his fast, a bomb was thrown. It injured nobody, but the minister of home affairs was fearful that Gandhi would be killed. He wanted everyone who attended the prayer meetings to be searched; Gandhi refused.

"If I have to die, I should like to die at the prayer meeting. You are wrong in believing that you can protect me from harm. God is my Protector," Gandhi told him.

Calcutta, shown here with dead bodies in the street, was the scene of the most violent clashes both before and during Indian independence. Gandhi was able to calm the city, but only by saying he would fast until peace was achieved.

This photo, taken the day before Gandhi's assassination, shows him with his great-nieces Manu and Abhu.

The death of Gandhi

When Gandhi was a young lawyer fighting for Indian rights in South Africa, he was attacked by fellow Indians. One Muslim Indian who suspected that he had betrayed the cause threatened to kill him. Gandhi was not dismayed. Death held no fear for him. At that time, Gandhi said, "Death is the appointed end of all life. To die by the hand of a brother rather than by disease . . . cannot be for me a matter of sorrow and if I am free from thought of anger or hatred against my assailant I know that will rebound to my eternal welfare."

Gandhi's thoughts about death were Hindu beliefs. He did not believe in a personal meeting with God; in fact, he believed that the self, the individual person, would disappear. He thought death was like the joining of streams and rivers with the sea.

On the last day of his life, Gandhi rose in the cold clear Delhi dawn at 3:00 A.M. Most of the day he worked, held meetings, and spent time in prayer. He was still at Birla House, where he had performed his final fast.

At about 5:00 P.M., after a meeting, Gandhi came hurriedly out of the house because he was a little late for evening prayers. Robert Stimson, a British correspondent who was there, said: "He was wearing his usual white loin cloth and a pair of sandals. He had thrown a shawl round his chest for it was getting chilly. His arms were resting lightly on the shoulders of two companions and he was smiling. There were only two or three hundred people in the garden and they pressed eagerly toward him as he climbed the steps leading to the small raised lawn where the congregation had gathered. As he got to the top of the steps and approached the crowd he took his arms from the shoulders of his friend and raised his hands in salutation. He was still smiling. A thick set man in his thirties I should say, and dressed in khaki was in the forefront of the crowd. He moved a step towards Mr. Gandhi, took out a revolver and fired several shots." Gandhi murmured "He Rama" (Oh God),

stood for a couple of seconds with blood oozing onto his white clothes, and then fell down dead.

Lord Mountbatten recalled later what it was like to receive the news of Gandhi's death. "I was absolutely numbed and petrified," he said. "I went round at once to Birla House. There was a large crowd around the house already and inside it most of the members of government—everyone in tears. Gandhi looked very peaceful in death, but I dreaded what his death might bring.

"As I went into the house where his body was lying, someone in the crowd shouted out: 'It was a Muslim who did it!' I turned immediately and said: 'You fool, don't you know it was a Hindu?'

"Of course I didn't know—no one knew at that stage. But I did know this, if it was a Muslim, we were lost. There would be civil war without fail. Thank God it wasn't!"

The assassin turned out to be a Hindu extremist— a young man from Poona, named Nathuram Godse,

On January 30, 1948, Gandhi was shot and killed as he was about to lead an evening prayer session for several hundred people. This scene, from the film Gandhi, *shows a re-creation of the garden where he was assassinated.*

सच पर विश्वास रखो
सच ही सोचो सच ही करो
BELIEVE IN TRUTH
THINK TRUT &
LIVE T UTH

There are statues in memory of Gandhi, such as this one in Delhi, throughout India.

who was later hanged, along with another conspirator. Five others were sentenced to life imprisonment.

Gandhi's funeral took place on the banks of the holy river Yamuna at Rajghat where a million people waited for the cortege. His son Ramdas set fire to Gandhi's funeral pyre, which burned for fourteen hours. Gandhi's ashes were then scattered in the sacred rivers of India and in the sea at Bombay.

Over the radio, Jawaharlal Nehru, now India's prime minister, had given the news of Gandhi's death to the Indian people shortly after the murder. He said, "The light has gone out of our lives and there is darkness everywhere and I do not know what to tell you and how to say it. Our beloved leader, Bapu as we call him, the Father of our Nation, is now no more."

Gandhi's gifts to India and the world

Nehru said, "The light has gone out, I said, and yet I was wrong. For the light that shone in this country was no ordinary light. The light that has illumined this country for this many years will illumine this country for many more years, and a thousand years later that light will be seen in this country, and the world will see it and it will give solace to innumerable hearts. For that light represented the living truth, and the eternal man was with us with his eternal truth reminding us of the right path, drawing us from error, taking this ancient country to freedom."

Mohandas Gandhi was the light of reason and the voice of love, tolerance, and peace in a century of violence. The little man in the loincloth left behind far more than his modest possessions. He left a legacy of nonviolent protest that has influenced thousands since his death.

Gandhi's great success in many ways was to prepare his people for independence. All his life, he had taught truthfulness and cleanliness. He taught the Hindus to take proper pride in their culture and traditions. He taught self-respect where Indians had been submissive under the yoke of the British Empire. By his example of courage and fearlessness, Gandhi taught his people to stand up for themselves.

Gandhi identified with the poor and they with him. He was loved by the factory workers, the peasants, and the depressed classes for whom he consistently fought. He won the affection of many Muslims for his efforts on their behalf. He came to embody the true spirit of India.

Gandhi visited the king of England at Buckingham Palace. The king asked him, "Mr.

In accordance with his beliefs, Gandhi left behind few possessions. Among them were an inexpensive watch, a pair of glasses, and a book of songs.

Gandhi is still regarded by many Indian people as the father of their nation and their greatest leader. People show their respect to his memory by leaving tributes at the place he was cremated (right).

....

"Between the two world wars, at the heyday of Colonialism, force reigned supreme. It had a suggestive power, and it was natural for the weaker to lie down before the stronger. "Then came Gandhi, chasing out of his country, almost singlehanded, the greatest military power on earth. He taught the world that there are higher things than force, higher even than life itself; he proved that force had lost its suggestive power."

—Albert Szent-Györgyi, Nobel laureate

....

....

"Gandhi was inevitable. If humanity is to progress, Gandhi is inescapable. He lived, thought and acted, inspired by a vision of humanity evolving toward a world of peace and harmony. We may ignore him at our own risk."

—Dr. Martin Luther King Jr.

....

Gandhi, how is India doing?" Pointing to his thin limbs and humble loincloth, Gandhi replied, "Look at me, and you will know from me what India is like." Perhaps this was the secret of Gandhi's power and his mass appeal. Many Indians looked upon him as a symbol of India. In his poverty and humility, he mirrored their lives. He was one of them.

Glossary

Ahimsa: The principle of nonviolence in all thoughts and actions and to all living creatures.
Ashram: A self-contained, usually religious, community.
Boer War: Fought in South Africa between the Boers and the British between 1899 and 1901.
Brahmacharya: A vow of perpetual celibacy.
Brahmin: A member of the highest (priestly) caste.
Caste system: A rigid system of hereditary social discrimination that divides people into four main groups: Brahmin, Kshatriya, Vaisya, and Sudra. Each group divides into thousands of smaller subgroups that originally related to occupation or rank. There are also the untouchables, who are at the lowest rank, and are not actually part of any caste.
Civil disobedience: A nonviolent way to try to achieve political goals by refusing to pay taxes or obey laws. This is the usual form of *satyagraha*.
Congress, Indian National: Founded to promote a role for native Indians in the government of India, it became increasingly politicized until it became the main organ of agitation for independence. It originally had Muslim participants as well, but is now a Hindu organization.

Dhoti: Loincloth.
Harijan: "Children of God" in Hindi; Gandhi's name for the untouchables.
Hartal: A sort of national strike, where shops and businesses close as a political protest, and the day is spent in fasting and other religious practices.
Hindu: A follower of Hinduism, one of the four major religions of the world, which is the main religion of India.
Khadi: Homespun cloth made on a hand wheel.
Kshatriya: A member of the second (or warrior) caste.
Mahatma: "Great Soul" in Sanskrit; a title given to Brahmin sages and bestowed on Gandhi in 1916.

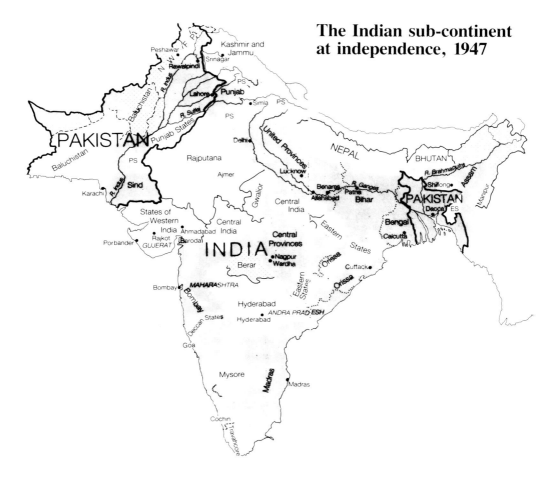

The Indian sub-continent at independence, 1947

Muslim: A follower of Islam, one of the four major religions of the world.

Pakistan: The two areas in the north of the Indian subcontinent where Muslims predominated. East Pakistan gained independence after a war in 1971 and is now called Bangladesh.

Partition: The splitting of the Indian subcontinent upon independence in 1947 into India and Pakistan. More than 12 million people fled across the new borders in one direction or the other.

Satyagraha: The force of "insisting on truth." The name "Gandhi" coined for his policy of nonviolent resistance to achieve a change in government or business policies.

Sudra: A member of the lowest (or worker) caste.

Untouchable: A person who was completely outside the caste system. Untouchables performed tasks such as road sweeping and lavatory cleaning that high-caste Hindus considered polluting.

Vaisya: A member of the third (professional or merchant) caste.

Viceroy: The governor of a country or province who acts for and rules in the name of the sovereign.

Important Dates

1869	Mohandas Karamchand Gandhi born on October 2 in Porbandar.
1882	Married to Kasturba.
1888	First son, Harilal, born. Gandhi sails to England to study law.
1891	Returns to India after being called to the bar.
1892	Second son, Manilal, is born.
1893	April: Sails to South Africa to work as a lawyer.
1896	Returns to India to get his family.
1897	Third son, Ramdas, is born.
1899–1901	Boer War takes place: Gandhi supports the British and organizes Ambulance Corps. His last son, Devadas, is born in 1900.
1904	Phoenix Farm purchased and Gandhi sets up his first ashram.
1906	Zulu Rebellion: Gandhi again organizes Ambulance Corps.
1908	First *satyagraha* campaign begins in South Africa.
1913	South Africa repeals some of the discriminatory legislation against Indian community.
1915	Gandhi returns to India and founds an ashram at Ahmedabad.
1919	Calls a hartal for March 30 and April 6. April 10: The massacre at Amritsar occurs.
1922	Jailed in March for six years (released in February 1924).
1928	Congress calls for independence for India.
1930	March: The Salt March to Dandi takes place. May: Gandhi is arrested just before congress organizes the demonstration at the Dharsana Saltworks.
1931	Gandhi released in January and leaves for Round Table Conference in London.
1932	On his return to India, Gandhi is rearrested (released in May 1933). September: Starts fast to the death to support untouchables.
1942	"Quit India" resolution passed by congress. Gandhi and other leaders arrested.
1944	February 22: Kasturba dies in prison. May: Gandhi released from prison.
1946	April: Jinnah calls for a separate Pakistan. August: Muslims massacre Hindus in Calcutta. Gandhi goes to the troubled areas.
1947	February: Lord Mountbatten appointed as last viceroy. August 15: Independence declared. September: Gandhi undertakes fast to the death against Hindu-Muslim violence.
1948	January 30: Gandhi assassinated.

Index